Olga Ermolitskaya

Accounting and control of investments in long-term assets

Olga Ermolitskaya

Accounting and control of investments in long-term assets

ScienciaScripts

Imprint
Any brand names and product names mentioned in this book are subject to trademark, brand or patent protection and are trademarks or registered trademarks of their respective holders. The use of brand names, product names, common names, trade names, product descriptions etc. even without a particular marking in this work is in no way to be construed to mean that such names may be regarded as unrestricted in respect of trademark and brand protection legislation and could thus be used by anyone.

Cover image: www.ingimage.com

This book is a translation from the original published under ISBN 978-620-2-07314-1.

Publisher:
Sciencia Scripts
is a trademark of
Dodo Books Indian Ocean Ltd. and OmniScriptum S.R.L publishing group

120 High Road, East Finchley, London, N2 9ED, United Kingdom
Str. Armeneasca 28/1, office 1, Chisinau MD-2012, Republic of Moldova, Europe
Printed at: see last page
ISBN: 978-620-7-79698-4

CONTENTS.

REFERENCE.

The volume of the scientific work is 57 pages of text typed on a computer. Bibliography is represented by 36 sources, 1 appendix.

Keywords: long-term assets, inventory, audit, classification of long-term assets, real estate, lease, IFRS, accounting, account, sub-account, fixed assets, depreciation.

Object of research: limited liability organization "Profitagro" of Starodorozhsky district of Minsk region.

Subject of the study: investments in non-current assets.

Purpose of work: to study the accounting and control of investments in long-term assets, to identify the existing shortcomings and develop ways to improve this area of accounting and control.

Research methods: comparisons, comparisons, balance links, calculation-analytical, monographic and calculation-constructive.

Researches and developments: as a result of the research the theoretical bases of investments in long-term assets are studied, accounting and control of investments in long-term assets on the example of LLC "Profitagro" of Starodorozhsky district of Minsk region are considered.

Degree of implementation: the directions of improving the accounting of investments in long-term assets in accordance with the requirements of international standards are tested on the example of LLC "Profitagro" Starodorozhsky district of Minsk region, as evidenced by the act of practical use.

Scope of application: the made proposals on improvement of accounting and control of investments in long-term assets can be further applied in LLC "Profitagro" of Starodorozhsky district of Minsk region and other agricultural organizations.

Significance of the work: specific proposals were made to improve the efficiency of the use of accounting and control of investments in long-term assets.

INTRODUCTION

The activity of agricultural organizations in the Republic of Belarus specializes in the production of crop and livestock products in connection with this requires constant modernization and renewal of fixed and working capital for more efficient operation of the national economic complex. For this purpose it is necessary to attract considerable funds from investors. Investments in the development of agriculture can come both in the form of state subsidies and from abroad. They can be attracted in different forms of investment: financial, intellectual and real.

Long-term assets are the tool that enables an enterprise to run its business. As a rule, in most manufacturing enterprises a significant part of property belongs to long-term assets. Their condition and effective use directly affects the final results of economic activity of organizations [3].

Effective functioning of organizations in the long term, ensuring high rates of their development and increasing competitiveness in modern market conditions are largely determined by the quality parameters of their investment activities. In this case, an important role is played by the reasonable optimization of the cost of investments in long-term assets, which subsequently forms the initial cost of fixed and intangible assets. In turn, this leads to a reduction in the amount of depreciation charges and, as a consequence, to an increase in efficiency, namely, to an increase in profit per 1 ruble of investments in long-term assets.

According to the preliminary data of the National Statistical Committee of the Republic of Belarus, investments in January-June 2017 in the real sector of the economy (except for banks) foreign investors invested IZE 4.9 billion [10].

The main investors of the organizations of the republic were business entities of the Russian Federation (39.6% of all incoming investments), the United Kingdom of Great Britain and Northern Ireland (28.3%), and Cyprus (7.4%).

The inflow of direct foreign investments amounted to FE 4.1 billion, or 83.1% of all foreign investments received. In January-June 2017, the organizations of the republic (except for banks) sent abroad investments worth FE 2.6 billion. Significant volumes of investments by the organizations of the republic were sent to economic entities of the Russian Federation (65.7% of all directed investments), Ukraine (17.1%), the United Kingdom of Great Britain and Northern Ireland (8%).Direct investments accounted for 93.7% of all directed investments abroad.

January 30, 2017. The Council of Ministers of the Republic of Belarus adopted Resolution No. 84 "On the issues of depreciation of fixed assets and intangible assets in 2017" aimed at creating conditions for the efficient operation of economic entities

[22].

In accordance with the document, organizations and individual entrepreneurs are granted the right not to charge depreciation on all or certain items of fixed assets and intangible assets used by them in entrepreneurial activity from 1 January to 31 December 2017. At the same time, this right does not apply to fixed assets used in the provision of housing, utilities and transport services to the population which are subsidized at the expense of budgetary funds.

According to the resolution, standard service lives and useful lives of fixed and intangible assets are extended for a period equal to the period in which depreciation was not charged.

The relevance of this paper is that the correctness of accounting of long-term assets at the enterprise is of great importance and to a certain extent affects the reliability of financial statements of a business entity. This paper considers the essence of investments in long-term assets, accounting and control over them, problems and ways to improve the accounting and control of investments in long-term assets in the context of convergence of national accounting standards for long-term assets with the requirements of International Financial Reporting Standards (hereinafter - IFRS).

The purpose of scientific work is to study the organization and methodology of accounting and control of investments in long-term assets and to develop ways to improve them in order to increase the efficiency of the use of the property of a business entity.

The main objectives of the study are:

- reflect the economic essence, content of investments in long-term assets, and their classification;

Identify problems and ways to improve the accounting of investments in long-term assets;

- study the organization of internal and external control over investments in long-term assets.

The object of research of this paper is investments in long-term assets in LLC "Profitagro" of Starodorozhsky district of Minsk region.

The subject of the study is the methodology of accounting and control of investments in long-term assets.

In the study of this topic the general scientific methods such as synthesis, analysis, comparison, description, generalization, analogy, induction, deduction, systematic approach were used. Along with these methods, theoretical aspects of accounting applied both in foreign countries and in our country were used in the study of the topic: the basic principles of accounting, qualitative characteristics of information of financial statements, considered in close interrelation, as well as the provisions of current legislation and IFRS.

Theoretical basis for writing the work were scientific works of scientists, developments of economists-practitioners, materials of periodicals, special methodological and educational literature on accounting by such scientists as Chechetkin A.S., Bepershch T.I., Kutselay E. V., Klippert E.N., Dalezkai T.A., manual of IFRS and others. V., Klippert E.N., Datskaya T.A., IFRS manual and others.

CHAPTER 1

THEORETICAL BASIS OF ACCOUNTING AND CONTROL OF INVESTMENTS IN LONG-TERM ASSETS PROFITAGRO LTD. OF STARODOROZHSKY DISTRICT OF MINSK REGION, MINSK OBLAST

1.1 Economic substance of investments in long-term assets and accounting objectives

Non-current assets are an essential element of the production process. They include assets that are intended for use in the organization's operations for a period of more than 12 months, or are to be disposed of or redeemed more than 12 months after the reporting date, or are not cash or cash equivalents [28].

Investments in non-current assets are the organization's investments in objects that will later be accepted for accounting purposes as fixed assets, investment real estate, intangible assets and other non-current assets.

Long-term assets of the organization include: fixed assets, intangible assets, income investments in tangible assets, equipment for installation and construction materials, long-term financial investments, as well as investments in long-term assets [11, p. 351].

Every organization owns property, which, according to the legislation, is recorded as an asset in the balance sheet. The main purpose of acquiring non-current assets is to use them in the process of production, provision of services or sale of goods, rather than for resale. Other purposes of non-current assets may also include leasing, use for administrative purposes and maintenance of fixed assets in working condition.

Long-term assets make up the bulk of all assets of enterprises and have a significant impact on the performance of the business entity.

According to the National Statistical Committee of the Republic of Belarus, in 2016 the initial value of fixed assets amounted to 205,627 million rubles, which is 18,135 million rubles more than in 2015 (187,492 million rubles). The share of accumulated depreciation in the initial value of fixed assets in the Republic of Belarus in 2016 amounted to 41.0%, which is 0.2% more than in 2015 (40.8%) [25].

A more complete and rational use of long-term assets of the organization contributes to the improvement of all its technical and economic indicators: increase in labor productivity, increase in stock productivity, increase in output, decrease in its cost, saving of investments in long-term assets. And in this case, in order to improve the efficiency of selection and implementation of management decisions, it is necessary to apply economic analysis.

6

In modern economics, accounting becomes an invaluable source of information for management and owners of an organization when forming prices and costs of products in order to qualitatively and comprehensively control the use of long-term assets and determine investment opportunities.

The majority of long-term assets are formed according to a single principle: their long-term participation in the production process (more than one year) and transfer of value to manufactured products by installments over several years. Therefore, the so-called long-term assets are constantly in the turnover of funds of the enterprise (organization). At the same time, they transfer their value to manufactured products (works, services) through depreciation charges. The cycle of this turnover is longer, but it is carried out constantly [30].

At the same time, non-current assets are classified as weakly liquid assets. This means that they can be converted into cash without significant losses only after significant periods of time (from six months and more). It is clear that fundamental property assets adapted to a certain type of business are much more difficult to sell on the market than, say, consumer goods or short-term assets (liquid products, inventories).

Long-term assets are also characterized by the fact that they are poorly managed operationally, as they have little variability in structure over short periods of time.

Thus, under long-term assets are understood assets that repeatedly participate in the business activities of the organization, gradually transfer their value to the newly created consumer value (manufactured products), have a service life of more than 1 year, are acquired not for sale but for use and have or do not have a physical form.

Closely related to the above concepts is the category of "investment" as it is essentially nothing but the use of capital to generate more money.

The economic category "investment management" has entered the domestic scientific turnover quite recently.

The most important factor in increasing the efficiency of investment use in the organization is a favorable investment climate, which is determined by the following conditions [33]: the possibility of equal stimulation of domestic and foreign investors, protection from expropriation, requisitions by the state; tax deferral for capital-intensive and intensive technologies; tax exemption for organizations and other new enterprises for several years, etc. The following conditions are also important.

Forms of investments in long-term assets are: creation of new production; acquisition of intangible assets; acquisition of organizations; expansion of organizations construction of additional production facilities at the existing organization (construction) in order to create additional or new production capacities; new construction; modernization - a set of measures to improve the technical and economic level on the basis of introduction of advanced equipment and technology, etc.

The Organization may invest in a portion of property, buildings, premises, equipment and other tangible assets in order to make them available for temporary use to generate income as investment property or under finance lease agreements.

For accounting purposes, investments in non-current assets are classified according to various features, which can be reviewed in Table 1.1.

Table 1.1 - Classification of investments in non-current assets by various characteristics

Classification features of investments in non-current assets	Types of investments in non-current assets
By reproductive structure	- investments in new construction; - in the expansion; - into reconstruction; technical re-equipment.
By purpose	- investments in non-current assets investments in construction of production facilities; - investments in non-production construction.
By economic sector	- investment in industry; - construction investments; - investments in agriculture; investments in transportation; - trading investments; - to health care; - investment in education.
By method of work execution	-executed by contracting; -executed by economic method.
By source of funding	- state support (means of the republican budget, means of local budgets, means of the innovation fund, etc.); - own sources (profit of the organization); - borrowed and attracted sources (bank loans, loans of various organizations).
By technological structure construction costs	- construction and installation work; -work on installation of equipment; - purchase of equipment requiring and not requiring installation provided for in construction estimates; - purchase of tools and inventory included in construction estimates;

	- other works and costs.
By the method of inclusion the costs that increase the value of the object of accounting	- *direct costs* - costs that can be directly attributed to a specific object of accounting at the time of their occurrence; - *indirect costs* - costs that cannot be directly attributed to a specific object of accounting at the time of their occurrence.

Note - author's elaboration

In accordance with the Instruction on the procedure for preparation of financial statements, approved by the Resolution of the Ministry of Finance of the Republic of Belarus dated 31.10.2011 No. 111, long-term assets also include "long-term accounts receivable" in addition to the above-mentioned items.

The main objectives of accounting for investments in long-term assets are [8]:

- correct classification of assets as non-current assets;

- timely revaluation of fixed assets and reflection of its results in the accounting accounts;

- proper choice of methods for valuation of long-lived assets;

- timely and accurate depreciation of fixed and intangible assets;

- correct and timely recording of additions and disposals of non-current assets and others.

- correct determination and reflection of the inventory value of fixed assets, land plots, natural resources, intangible assets;

- development of rational document flow for accounting of investments in long-term assets;

- timely, complete and reliable reflection of expenses on investments in long-term assets in primary documents and in accounting by their types and cost items;

- control over availability and utilization of sources of financing of long-term investments, etc.

Thus, long-term assets constitute the main part of all assets of enterprises and have a significant impact on the results of the economic entity's activity, and investments in long-term assets represent a set of costs allocated to the creation of new, technical re-equipment, reconstruction of existing fixed assets.

1.2 Essence and significance of control over investments in non-current assets

The proportionality of the sources of financing of investments in long-term assets and the volume of completed construction and installation works, costs for the acquisition of fixed and intangible assets provides financial stability of the organization and preservation of own funds in turnover [27].

Given the importance of the economic concept "investments in long-term assets" for both the economic entity and the economy as a whole, the audit of this area of accounting work allows solving a number of global tasks. Namely, the audit reveals the compliance of operations with investments in non-current assets with the regulatory and legal framework of the Republic of Belarus.

Considering the control of investments in long-term assets, it should be noted that the organization should conduct an audit of the general ledger, disposal of fixed assets, verification of the procedure of annual inventory of fixed assets, verification of the correctness of depreciation on fixed assets, audit of accounting of income investments in tangible assets, and verification of investments in long-term assets. In each item of the conducted audit, violations are indicated, as well as recommendations for their correction. All of the above is reflected in the Report on the results of the audit of the organization [12, p. 86].

The essence of control over investments in long-term assets is to establish the efficiency of the use of funds allocated for investments in long-term assets; timeliness, completeness and reliability of cost accounting for these investments.

Depending on the form of investment, investments in long-term assets are subdivided into: acquisition (purchase) of objects; creation of objects, including through research and development and experimental technological works and others.

On this basis, investments in non-current assets are tested in two ways:

- verification of investments in long-term assets related to new construction, reconstruction, expansion, technical re-equipment of existing fixed assets;

- verification of operations on acquisition (purchase) of fixed assets.

The control objectives for investments in long-lived assets include:

-supply of investments with design and estimate documentation;

- fulfillment of the capital investment plan;

- timely, complete and reliable reflection of costs by types and objects of capital investments;

- the correctness of determining the inventory value of construction objects put into operation and their entry into the fixed assets of the organization;

- correctness of organization of accounting' and reporting on investment activities.

The objectives of accounting and control of investments in non-current assets are [29]:

- timely, complete and accurate reflection of all expenses incurred by type and accounted for objects;

- ensuring control over the progress of works, commissioning of production facilities and other fixed and intangible assets;

- correct determination and recording of the initial cost of fixed assets, land plots, natural resources and intangible assets;

- control over the availability and use of sources of financing for long-term investments.

The sources of information for checking investments in long-term assets are: contracts of contracting and equipment supply; title lists of construction sites; logbook of completed construction and installation works (Form No. C-6); acceptance certificates of completed construction and installation works (Form No. C-2); certificates of cost of completed works and costs (Form No. C-3); primary documents on accounting of labor and its payment, consumption of materials; accounting registers - journal-orders No. 10-C, 11-C, statements No. 5-C "Settlements with customers (general contractors) and contractors (subcontractors) for work performed or the corresponding machine-grams; statistical reporting "Report on commissioning of facilities and performance of contract work (form No. 1 -KS (urgent)), etc.". [5, c. 116].

Of particular importance in the management of investments in long-term assets is the control system that ensures the completeness and correctness of future actions aimed at reducing costs and improving production efficiency. They are grouped into controlled and uncontrolled. Controllable assets are long-term assets that the head of the structural unit can directly control or have a significant influence on them. In turn, non-controlled long-term assets do not depend on the activities of the organization's structural subdivisions (e.g., revaluation of fixed assets resulting in an increase in depreciation charges, changes in prices for fuel and energy resources, etc.) and, as a result, the head of the structural subdivision cannot control or influence them.

The auditor should pay special attention to verifying the correctness of the loss of accounting for the costs of investments in long-term assets in leased fixed assets provided for in the lease agreement. They may be made at the expense of the lessor as a reduction of the lessees' rent or at the expense of the lessee. If the agreement provides for capital investments in leased fixed assets at the expense of the lessee, they are transferred to the lessor free of charge at the end of the lease term. The transfer is formalized by accounting records on gratuitous transfer of fixed assets. Completed capital investments in leased fixed assets are accounted for in the relevant accounts of subsection 12 "Fixed assets" and are reflected in the lessor's balance sheet as additional value of leased fixed assets.

The audit of investments in long-term assets includes the audit [31, p.25]:

- fixed assets (verification of the correctness of attributing objects to fixed assets, cost estimation of fixed assets, accrual and reflection in the accounting records of depreciation and impairment of fixed assets, carrying out and reflection in the accounting records of revaluation, reflection in the accounting records of receipt, disposal, internal movement of fixed assets, costs of their reconstruction (modernization, restoration));

- intangible assets (verification of the correctness of attributing objects to intangible assets, their cost estimation, correctness of accrual and accounting of amortization and impairment of intangible assets, correctness of accounting of receipt and disposal of intangible assets);

- income investments in tangible assets (verification of correctness of accounting of business operations with investment real estate, financial rent (leasing) items).

The inventories and costs of the audited entity are subject to mandatory audit [31, p. 26]:

- correctness of assignment of objects to materials and separate items within the means of turnover, correctness of their cost estimation, recording in the accounting records of receipt, release for production or transfer for operation, other disposal of materials and separate items within the means of turnover, as well as correctness of formation and use of reserves for decrease in the cost of inventories;

- correctness of accounting of finished products output and its realization, receipt and realization of goods, accounting of expenses for realization of products, goods, works, services;

- correctness of formation and reflection in accounting of direct costs of the main and auxiliary productions, general production and general economic costs, costs of servicing productions and farms, losses from rejects, correctness of evaluation and reflection in accounting of unfinished production, determination of the cost of finished products.

The problem of accounting for investments in long-term assets is the inattention of managers to accounting. It is necessary to introduce additional control over accounting for long-term assets on the part of the company's management. This means familiarization of the manager with accounting documents, study of regulations in force in this area. Such an approach will make it possible to spend funds more rationally on the acquisition of long-term assets and increase the discipline of their use by the employees of the enterprise. In addition, it is necessary to analyze the efficiency of the use of long-term assets based on accounting data under the direct control of the head of the enterprise. In this case, the manager will receive a more complete picture of the state of affairs at the enterprise.

In our opinion, separate attention should also be paid to accounting statements of enterprises related to accounting for investments in long-term assets. Correctly determine the methods of accounting accepted in the formation of the accounting policy of the organization.

In the practice of organizations, there are operations involving the sale of long-term investments with a long-term, multi-year installment payment (leasing). When carrying out operations of sale of long-term investments in installments for a long period of time, there is a problem of reflection in the accounting of income and expenses of actions on this operation. Since cash receipts will be carried out for a long period of time and there is no final guarantee that all cash will be received, the recognition in accounting of income from the sale of such assets in installments should be postponed [12, p. 87].

Thus, control over investments in non-current assets is the most important part of accounting and for the organization as a whole, because control of this area of accounting work allows to solve a number of global tasks. To be more precise, the control activities reveal the compliance of operations with investments in non-current assets with the regulatory and legal framework of the Republic of Belarus. During the audit it is possible to identify violations, if any, and safely correct them without many consequences for the organization.

1.3 Accounting and control of investments in non-current assets in accordance with international standards

Various standards are being developed in order to harmonize the reporting indicators of the Republic of Belarus with international standards.

On December 19, 2015, the Regulation on the Procedure for the Implementation of International Financial Reporting Standards and their Explanations adopted by the International Accounting Standards Foundation in the Republic of Belarus approved by the Resolution of the Council of Ministers of the Republic of Belarus and the National Bank of the Republic of Belarus No. 1043/20 dd. 15.12.2015 came into force [14].

International Financial Reporting Standards are a set of documents (standards and interpretations) that regulate the rules for preparing financial statements required by external users for making economic decisions in the organization.

Accounting and control of investments in non-current assets is regulated by such international standards as IFRS 5 "Non-current Assets Held for Sale and Discontinued Operations", IAS 16 "Property, Plant and Equipment", IAS 17 "Leases", IAS 20 "Accounting for Government Grants and Disclosure of Government Assistance", IAS 23 "Borrowing Costs", IAS 40 "Investment Property".

The objective of IFRS 5 is to determine how to account for assets held for sale and how to present and disclose information about discontinued operations. Specifically, this IFRS 5 requires [19]:

- that assets that meet the criteria to be classified as held for sale are measured at the lower of their carrying amount and fair value less costs to sell and depreciation on such assets is discontinued;

- that assets that meet the criteria to be classified as held for sale are presented separately in the statement of financial position and the results of discontinued operations are presented separately in the statement of comprehensive income.

The measurement requirements in this IFRS 5 apply to all recognized non-current assets and disposal groups (as described in paragraph 4), except for those assets listed in paragraph 5 that continue to be required to be measured in accordance with that standard.

The measurement provisions of this IFRS 5 do not apply to the following assets that are subject to the listed standards, either as separate assets or as part of a disposal group:

- deferred tax assets (IAS 12 Income Taxes);

- assets arising from employee benefits (IAS 19 Employee Benefits);

- financial assets within the scope of IFRS 9 Financial Instruments;

- long-lived assets that are accounted for in accordance with the fair value model presented in IAS 40 Investment Property;

- non-current assets that are measured at fair value less costs to sell in accordance with IAS 41 Agriculture;

- rights arising from insurance contracts as defined in IFRS 4 Insurance Contracts.

IFRS 5 does not require an entity to depreciate a non-current asset while it is classified as held for sale or while it is part of a disposal group classified as held for sale. Interest and other expense relating to the liabilities of a disposal group classified as held for sale must continue to be recognized.

In accordance with IAS *16 fixed* assets are assets intended for use in the production or supply of goods and services, for leasing to third parties or for administrative purposes for more than one period [15].

The purpose of MCBY(IAS) 16 is to define the accounting treatment of property, plant and equipment to provide users of financial statements with information about investments in property, plant and equipment and changes in those investments. The main issues in accounting for property, plant and equipment are recognition of assets, determination of their carrying amount, depreciation charges and impairment losses.

IAS 16 does not apply to:

- property, plant and equipment held for sale in accordance with IFRS 5;

- biological assets related to agricultural activities in accordance with IAS 41;

- recognizing and measuring mineral exploration and evaluation assets in accordance with IFRS 6 Exploration for and Evaluation of Mineral Resources;

- mineral rights and mineral reserves, such as oil, natural gas and similar non-recoverable resources.

IAS 16 applies to property, plant and equipment used to develop and provide assets within the scope of IAS 41 and IFRS 6 and mineral rights.

Accounting for property, plant and equipment under IFRS is regulated by a separate standard IAS 16 "Property, Plant and Equipment". In the Belarusian legislation this object of accounting is regulated by the Instruction on Accounting for Fixed Assets approved by the Resolution of the Ministry of Finance of the Republic of Belarus No. 26 dated April 30, 2012.

In accordance with IAS 16 "Property, Plant and Equipment", property, plant and equipment are tangible fixed assets with a useful life of more than 1 year that are used: for the production or supply of goods and services; for leasing to other companies; or for administrative purposes.

An item of property, plant and equipment under IAS 16 is recognized as an asset if:

- it is probable that future economic benefits associated with the asset will flow to the entity;

- the value of the asset can be measured reliably.

Thus, IAS 16 requires a fairly detailed description of the accounting and valuation methods used for property, plant and equipment. The explanatory note to the financial statements should include the following information for each group of property, plant and equipment:

- the method of subsequent evaluation used;

- the depreciation method used;

- expected useful life or depreciation rate;

- the accounting value of the fixed asset and accumulated depreciation at the beginning and end of the reporting period;

- analysis of changes in the balances of fixed assets and accumulated depreciation: new acquisitions and write-offs, revaluations, internal transfers, reclassifications, adjustments of errors, exchange rate differences, impairment losses and reversals, changes in depreciation charges and other significant changes.

In addition, the report should disclose information on the following facts, if any:

- any restrictions on ownership and the fact that assets are pledged as collateral;

- accounting policy regarding the capitalization of restoration and reconstruction costs of property and equipment;

- costs of property, plant and equipment, including construction in progress;

- amounts of unpaid commitments to purchase property, plant and equipment;

- data on the use of discounted cash flows to determine the recoverable amount of assets.

According to IAS 17, a *lease is a* contract in which the lessor conveys to the lessee, in exchange for a rent or a series of payments, the right to use an asset for an agreed period of time [16].

IAS 17 applies to the accounting for all leases, except for leases for the exploration or use of minerals, oil, natural resources and other renewable resources, and licensing agreements for films, videos, plays, manuscripts, patents and copyrights.

IAS 17 is not applicable to the valuation:

- real estate held by the lessee and accounted for as investment property (IAS 40);

- investment property provided by lessors under investment leases (IAS 40);

- biological assets held by the lessee under finance leases (IAS 41);

- biological assets provided by lessors under operating leases.

IAS 17 also addresses leaseback transactions in which the seller of the asset is the lessee. If the leaseback transaction results in a finance lease, the excess of the proceeds over the carrying amount of the asset is recognized as deferred income in the books of the seller-lessee and included in the income statement over the lease term. If the leaseback transaction results in an operating lease, the accounting treatment depends on the relationship between the sale price and the fair value of the asset:

- if the sales price equals the fair value of the asset, a gain or loss on the sale is recognized immediately;

- if the sale price is below fair value, a gain or loss on the sale is recognized immediately, except that any offsetting loss is offset by future lease payments at a price below market value. The loss is recognized on a pro rata basis over the lease payments over the period of use of the asset;

- if the sales price is higher than the fair value, the excess is recognized in income over the useful life of the asset.

If, under an operating lease, the fair value of the asset at the time of sale and leaseback is lower than its carrying amount, the difference is recognized as a loss.

In accordance with IAS 20, *government grants* are government assistance in the form of a transfer of resources to an entity in exchange for past or future compliance with certain conditions related to the entity's operations. Government grants do not include forms of government assistance that cannot be reasonably estimated, as well as transactions with the government that do not differ from the company's normal operations [17].

IAS 20 applies to the accounting for and disclosure of government grants and other forms of state aid.

IAS 20 does not disclose:

- special problems arising from the accounting for government grants in the financial statements that reflect the effects of price changes or in supplementary information of a similar nature;

- information on government assistance provided to the company in the form of benefits in determining taxable income or benefits determined or limited based on the amount of income taxes owed (e.g., temporary exemption from income taxes), investment and tax credits, accelerated depreciation allowances, reduced income tax rates;

- state participation in the management of the company;

- government grants considered within the scope of IAS 41.

Disclosures in the financial statements in accordance with IAS 20 "Accounting for Government Grants and Disclosure of Government Assistance" the following should be disclosed:

- accounting policies adopted for government grants, including the presentation methods used in the financial statements;

- the nature and amount of government grants recognized in the financial statements and an indication of other forms of government assistance from which the company has directly benefited;

- unfulfilled conditions and other contingent events related to state aid that has been recognized.

According to IAS 23, *borrowing costs are* interest and other expenses directly related to the use of borrowed funds [18].

The objective of IAS 23 is to determine the accounting method for recognizing borrowing costs. IAS 23 requires that borrowing costs be recognized as an expense in the reporting period. As an alternative method, IAS 23 permits capitalization of borrowing costs associated with the acquisition, construction or production of a qualifying asset. IAS 23 is applicable to the accounting for borrowing costs.

Borrowing costs that are directly attributable to the acquisition, construction or production of a qualifying asset shall be capitalized as part of the cost of that asset. The amount of costs eligible for capitalization is determined in accordance with IAS 23.

IAS 23 provides that difficulties in determining a direct link between specific borrowings and a qualifying asset arise if an entity's financing activities are centrally coordinated. Problems may arise if a group of companies borrows at different interest rates and allocates those funds on a different basis to entities within the group. The situation is further complicated by fluctuations in exchange rates when foreign currency loans are used in the context of significant inflation.

Thus, IAS 23 considers the temporary investment of borrowed funds raised for the acquisition of a qualifying asset. It is noted that in determining the amount of borrowing costs to be capitalized, income received as a result of investing the funds is excluded.

IAS 40 Investment Property specifies the accounting for investment property and related disclosure requirements. It should be noted that this Standard does not address the issues associated with IAS 17, including [20]:

- The classification of leases into finance leases and operating leases;

- Recognition of rental income from investment property;

- An estimate of the interest income reported in the lessee's financial statements;

- The measurement of the net investment in the finance lease in the lessor's financial statements;

- accounting for sale and leaseback transactions;

- disclosure of finance and operating leases.

Real estate investments represent land or buildings used (by title or under a finance lease) to earn rentals, for capital appreciation or both.

IAS 40 does not apply to properties that are owner-occupied, under construction and to be used in the future as a real estate investment or held for sale in the ordinary course of business.

A choice of fair value or cost accounting is available:

- fair value accounting: investment property is measured at fair value through profit or loss;

- cost accounting: investments in real estate are measured at amortized cost less accumulated impairment losses. The fair value of real estate investments shall be disclosed.

The accounting option selected must be applied to all real estate investments.

If the fair value method of accounting has been selected, but at the time of acquisition of a particular item it becomes clear that it is not practicable to determine fair value on a recurring basis, the item is accounted for at cost, and this option must be exercised until the item is disposed of.

IAS 40 permits a change from one option to another if it will improve presentation (which is unlikely in the case of a change from fair value to cost accounting).

A lessee's rights under an operating lease may be treated as an investment in real estate provided that the lessee applies the fair value option in accordance with IAS 40. In this case, the lessee accounts for the rights under the operating lease as if it were a finance lease [36, 101 p.].

IAS 16 Property, Plant and Equipment applies to owner-occupied property that is owned, and IFRS 16 applies to owner-occupied property that is held by a lessee as a right-of-use asset.

Assets that are not real estate investments and are not within the scope of IAS 40 include [6]:

- items held for sale in the ordinary course of business or assets under construction and under reconstruction held for sale (accounted for in accordance with IAS 2 Inventories);

- owner-occupied real estate (reported in accordance with IAS 16 Property, Plant and Equipment);

- construction in progress or real estate under reconstruction on behalf of third parties (the provisions of IAS 11 Construction Contracts apply).

In the balance sheet, investment properties are reported as assets in a separate line item at fair value or cost less accumulated depreciation and impairment losses.

Based on the above, it can be concluded that each real estate investment property is unique in its kind and each sale and purchase transaction is subject to significant negotiations. As a result, fair value measurement does not promote comparability of information because fair value cannot be determined with sufficient reliability. Valuation at amortized cost is more consistent and less subjective.

Thus, having studied the theoretical basis of accounting and control of investments in long-term assets, we would like to note that in most production enterprises, as well as in the studied LLC "Profitagro", a significant part of the property belongs to long-term assets, and the overwhelming part of investments in long-term assets are fixed assets. Fixed assets are one of the most important factors of any production. Their condition and effective utilization directly affects the final results of economic activity of enterprises.

CHAPTER 2

ACCOUNTING FOR INVESTMENTS IN LONG-TERM ASSETS AND ITS IMPROVEMENT AT PROFITAGRO LTD.

2.1 Documentation of investments in non-current assets

It is known that one of the conditions for the principle of validity of acceptance of a business transaction for accounting and its reliability is documentary support of the transaction. A transaction is accepted for accounting in the presence of properly executed primary documents.

Depending on the sources of formation and characteristics of the objects of investments in long-term assets can be formalized by different primary documents [4]:

- act of acceptance-transfer of fixed assets is a unified document (prepared in accordance with the resolution of the Ministry of Finance of RB dated 22.04.2011 № 23), TN, TTN, as well as acts of work performed, insurance policies and other documents on the basis of which the costs are attributed to increase the cost of fixed assets;

- act of acceptance and transfer of intangible assets, as well as acts of work performed, insurance policies and other documents on the basis of which expenses may be attributed to increase in the value of intangible assets;

- act of transfer of animals to the main herd;

- act of property write-off (in case of physical wear and tear, loss (destruction) due to extraordinary circumstances);

- act of acceptance-transfer of groups of fixed assets;

- invoice for internal transfer of fixed assets;

- act of acceptance of repaired, reconstructed, modernized, retrofitted fixed assets;

- act on installation, start-up and dismantling of construction machines;

- act of acceptance-transfer of perennial plantings and their commissioning;

- leasing agreement.

Investments in non-current assets of separate accounting objects include equipment to be installed and construction materials. The cost of equipment requiring installation, as well as construction materials is estimated at the amount of actual costs of their acquisition without value added tax [7].

Receipt of equipment requiring installation is formalized by a bill of lading or customs cargo declaration. Acceptance of equipment for completeness is carried out by a special

21

commission with the participation of a representative of the contractor. The equipment may be delivered to the warehouse or construction site with a certificate of acceptance of the equipment.

Transfer of the equipment from the developer's warehouse to the contractor for subsequent assembly and installation is formalized by a certificate of acceptance of transfer of the equipment for installation. The assembled equipment is handed back to the customer under the act of acceptance of completed work.

All the above documents are also used in the organization under study, Profitagro LLC, except for the act of acceptance-transfer of intangible assets.

Many shortcomings in the organization of documentary support of the management apparatus are associated with the fuzzy organization of document movement.

In our opinion, one of the disadvantages in filling out documents in the organization is that the organization uses the traditional card form of document accounting. However, one of its serious disadvantages is the lack of certain guarantee in the safety of record cards in the file cabinet and the possibility of their easy substitution. In this connection, there is a need to keep track of the cards and maintain a special record form for this purpose.

Account 07 "Equipment for installation and construction materials" is intended for generalization of information on the availability and movement of equipment requiring installation and intended for installation in the objects under construction, as well as construction materials used by the customer, developer in the performance of construction and other special installation works and subsequently included in the initial cost of the construction object and (or) equipment for installation in LLC Profitagro. Equipment requiring installation and construction materials in the balance sheet and in current accounting are valued at the actual cost of their acquisition (including all delivery and acquisition costs).

The following standardized documents are drawn up when carrying out construction and installation works, which are approved by the resolution of the Ministry of Architecture and Construction of RB from 29.04.2011 № 13 "On establishing the forms of primary documents in construction" [23]:

- C-2 "Certificate of acceptance of construction and other special installation works".

- C-22-"Certificate of Transfer of Facility Not Completed";

- "Act on the transfer of costs incurred in the creation of an engineering and (or) transportation infrastructure facility".

- C-1 "Defect Report."

- C-3 "Statement of Cost of Work and Expenditures".

- C-5 "Certificate of Occupancy of Non-Title Temporary Building and Structure".

- C-6 "Certificate of dismantling of non-title temporary building and structure

- C-11 "Act on defects, deficiencies

- C-12 "Construction Vehicle Rental Time Statement."

- C-13 "Bill of lading for internal transfer".

- C-15 "Register of acceptance certificates of completed works".

- C-16 "Bill of lading for transfer of technical documentation".

- C-17 "Act for transfer of costs incurred in the creation of an object

- C-18 "Shift Report."

When construction is carried out by economic method, employees of the given organization are involved in the execution of works, their own production base is created, construction materials, machines and mechanisms are purchased. The progress of works and control over their implementation are carried out by capital construction departments. They accept the completed works and sign the relevant documents.

Construction engineers, as well as construction supervisors (foremen) are responsible for accounting of the volumes of completed construction and installation works. Every month on the 1st day of the month following the reporting month, the foreman measures (counts) the completed construction and erection works for each type of works and reflects the obtained data in the register of completed works.

Upon completion of construction, the total scope and estimated cost of the work actually performed as a whole shall be determined.

In order to determine the scope of work performed and the estimated cost, an inventory report of construction and assembly work in progress is prepared. The act is prepared by the foreman indicating the percentage of readiness of the object. In turn, the percentage of readiness determines the volume and cost of construction and installation work in progress.

Write-off of materials and structures used for construction and installation works is made on the basis of the foreman's report. At the end of the month, the foreman submits to the construction engineer the Material Report and the Report on the consumption of basic materials in construction in comparison with the production norms, which after verification of material consumption norms are transferred to the accounting department for processing.

To account for costs associated with investments in long-term assets from the beginning of construction until the commissioning of the facility, Profitagro LLC uses account 08 "Investments in long-term assets" sub-account 08.9.1 "Costs of construction and creation of fixed assets". Accounting of construction and installation works performed by economic method is carried out at the estimated cost of objects and their actual cost.

In accounting, construction costs are summarized by the following items: design and survey work; materials, construction structures and details; costs of operating construction machinery and mechanisms; basic wages of workers; overhead costs. The list of items and the procedure for allocation of overhead costs are determined by the accounting policy of the organization.

When using own or leased machines and mechanisms, the costs of their operation are accounted for in account 25 "General production costs", sub-account "Maintenance and operation of equipment". Own costs are also accounted for by cost items and by types of construction equipment (tower cranes, excavators, bulldozers, etc.).

Equipment operating expenses are allocated based on the number of machine shifts (machine days) worked at the facilities.

Overhead costs are costs associated with the management, maintenance and organization of construction. These include

- administrative and economic expenses - expenses on maintenance of the technical control and supervision group, OCS of the organization;

-expenses for construction workers' services - expenses for labor protection and safety, sanitary and welfare services, etc.

-expenses for organization of work at construction sites - expenses for maintenance of watch and fire guards, temporary structures, fixtures and devices.

Overheads are allocated between types of work and capital expenditure items in two stages. In the first stage, overheads are allocated between construction and installation works in proportion to the estimated amounts of these costs for the work performed. In the second stage, overheads are allocated to construction projects in proportion to the amounts of direct costs. After allocation, the costs are included in the cost of construction projects under "Overheads".

Investments in non-current assets are accounted for by the organization that carries out construction for itself and finances it. When making investments in non-current assets using a contractual method of work, a developer concludes a contract with a contractor. If the volume of investments is significant, the organization establishes a capital construction department (department). When building a new organization, the developer is the directorate of the organization under construction.

Prior to the start of construction, the developer organization enters into an agreement with a design organization for the preparation of design and estimate documentation.

An integral part of the design documentation is a summary estimate. This is the main document determining the cost of construction. The customer concludes a contract with a construction organization, which will be the general contractor for the entire construction period.

When work is carried out by contract, the developer does not need to keep records of costs by item and element. Such accounting is performed by the construction organization.

The developer organization records the estimated (contractual) cost of work performed by the contractor and accepted for payment. The procedure for settlements between the developer and the contractor is determined by the terms of the contract bidding or by agreement of the parties and is set out in the construction contract. Settlements may be made on a monthly basis for the volume of work actually performed or for a completed stage of construction work. In this case, the contractor shall prepare a Statement of Cost of Completed Construction Work, where it indicates the estimated cost of completed work to be paid for.

When starting to review investments in non-current assets, it is necessary to establish how the investments are realized.

At the contract method of construction LLC "Profitagro" makes settlements with the contractor organization at the estimated cost of the completed construction of the object on the basis of duly drawn up and approved acceptance certificate, cost control here is not difficult, but it is important to prevent the fact of payment to the contractor of amounts not provided for by the estimate, including through the enrollment of construction workers of the contractor organization at the enterprise and unjustified payment of unearned amounts to them. When developing investments by the contracting method, it is necessary to check the correctness of recording costs according to the data of primary documents. It should be borne in mind that the developer (investor), when carrying out work by contract, recognizes costs at the estimated (contractual) cost of the work performed.

In the course of the audit, the fulfillment of the plan of construction and installation works by objects, stages, complexes to be delivered to customers in the current year, by the total volume of contract works and contractors is thoroughly checked. If the plan of contracting works by the involved organizations is not fulfilled, the data on the corresponding subcontracting organizations are analyzed and the reasons for its non-fulfillment are found out. It should be borne in mind that the advance of the plan on the total volume of work compared to the plan of commissioning of production capacities and facilities causes the growth of unfinished production, dispersion of material and labor resources on the objects.

The inspector should also establish whether the construction and installation works envisaged at the time of execution of the act of acceptance into operation of the facilities were fully completed, whether construction and installation works were not carried out on certain facilities after they were put into operation. Attention should be paid to the periods of work performance.

Thus, we would like to note that accounting in LLC "Profitagro" is an orderly system of collection, registration and generalization of information in monetary terms about the obligations of the organization, property and their movement by means of solid, continuous documentation of all business operations. In our opinion, one of the main tasks of accounting is the correct, timely documentation and maintenance of operations on accounting and control of investments in long-term assets.

2.2 Synthetic and analytical accounting of investments in non-current assets

All types of long-term investments in agricultural organizations are accounted for on account 08 "Investments in long-term assets".

Account 08 "Investments in long-term assets" is intended to reflect information on the organization's investments in objects that will be subsequently accepted for accounting as fixed assets, intangible assets, investment real estate, other long-term assets, including the costs of forming the main herd of productive and working livestock (except for live poultry, fur animals, rabbits, bee families, service dogs, experimental animals, which are accounted for as inventories).

The following sub-accounts can be opened to account 08 "Investments in long-term assets" [35, p. 258]:

- 08-1 "Acquisition and Establishment of Fixed Assets."

- 08-2 "Acquisition and Establishment of Investment Real Estate."

- 08-3 "Acquisition of finance lease (leasing) items";

- 08-4 "Acquisition and Creation of Intangible Assets."

- 08-5 "Acquisition and Creation of Other Long-Lived Assets."

In LLC Profitagro accounting of investments in long-term assets is carried out on account 08 "Investments in long-term assets" with available sub-accounts:

- 08.1.1. - "Acquisition of fixed assets. Formation of the main herd";

- 08.9.1. - "Costs of construction and establishment of fixed assets".

In the analyzed organization on sub-account 08-1-1 "Acquisition of fixed assets.

Formation of the main herd" account for the costs of erection of buildings and structures, installation of equipment for installation and other costs directly related to the acquisition of fixed assets. Also on this sub-account in LLC "Profitagro" the actual costs of formation of the main herd due to the transfer of young stock raised in the farm are accounted as well. During the year when transferring to the main herd of young animals born in previous years, the cost is then determined based on the weight of animals and the planned cost of 1 kg of live weight.

Thus, during the year in LLC "Profitagro" various operations on account 08-1-1 "Acquisition of fixed assets. Formation of the main herd", which can be seen in Table 2.2.1 and 2.2.2.

During the year various equipment, machinery, tools were purchased in the organization, some of them can be seen in Table 2.1.

Table 2.1 - Correspondences on account 08-1-1 "Acquisition of fixed assets. Formation of the main herd" in LLC "Profitagro" for January-August 2017.

№ n/a	Content of business transaction	Debit	Credit	Amount
1.	Recorded the initial cost of the MT7-160-4UKh compressor purchased by the organization when it was put into operation	01-1	08-1-1	2 880,00
2.	Recorded the purchase price of MTT-4 U mineral fertilizer application machines purchased by the organization when put into operation	01-1	08-9-1	16 800,00

The organization Profitagro LLC received fixed assets during the year as a result of accepted young cattle. The following accounting records are made in accounting, which can be considered in Table 2.2.

Table 2.2 - Correspondences on account 08-1-1 "Acquisition of fixed assets. Formation of the main herd" in LLC "Profitagro" for January-August 2017.

No. n/a	Content of business transaction	Debit	Credit	Amount
1.	Cows transferred to the main herd for breeding and fattening	08-1-1	11-1	500 639,26
2.	Cows accepted as property, plant and equipment at purchase cost were recognized at cost	01-1	08-1-1	779 579,11

Sub-account 08-1-1 "Acquisition of fixed assets. Formation of the main herd" accounts for the costs of erection of buildings and structures, installation of equipment, the cost of equipment transferred for installation and other costs depending on the method of construction investments in long-term assets and related costs are accounted for by the developer (customer), i.e. the organization that carries out construction for itself and finances it.

The costs of construction and creation of fixed assets in LLC Profitagro are recorded on sub-account 08-9-1 "Costs of construction and creation of fixed assets". Accounting records on this sub-account are given for June 2017, which can be reviewed in Table 2.3.

Table 2.3 - Correspondences on sub-account 08-9-1 "Costs of construction and creation of fixed assets" for June 2017.

№ n/a	Content of business transaction	Debit	Credit	Amount
1.	Property, plant and equipment acquired and put into operation as a result of construction	01-1	08-9-1	149 720,36
2.	Reflected initial value of the barn created and put into operation	01	08-9-1	24 331,72
3.	Services of third-party organizations on territory improvement were written off	08-9-1	60	38 744,69

The balance (debit) on sub-account 08-1-1 "Acquisition of fixed assets. Formation of the main herd" shows the cost of construction in progress.

According to the method of production of construction works there are construction carried out by *contracting and economic methods.*

At *contracting method* construction and installation works are performed by specialized contracting construction and installation organizations. General contracting organizations carry out general construction works, are responsible to customers (agricultural organizations) for all construction works and commissioning. *Subcontracting* organizations perform separate types of construction works for the general contractor. The basis of relations between customers and general contractor is the general contract, and relations between general contractor and subcontractor - the subcontractor's contract.

Settlements between the customer and the contractor are made at estimated (contractual) prices for finished construction products (start-up complexes, industrial and social facilities, etc.).

In case of the contractor method of construction, the customer keeps records separately for each object under construction with one complex item "Works performed by the contractor". Upon completion of the construction of the object, the developer determines its inventory value, and the State Acceptance Commission accepts the object into operation and draws up a certificate of acceptance of the transfer of fixed assets.

If there are several parts of the facility, the acceptance certificates for construction and other special installation works shall specify the cost of construction works for each part of the facility.

If, in accordance with a construction contract, the customer is fully or partially responsible for providing construction materials, the customer is responsible for including the cost of materials used by the contractor in the construction costs. In accordance with the technological structure of costs, the cost of the customer's materials used by the contractor to perform construction work is included in the cost of construction and installation work or in the cost of equipment installation work.

For the purpose of forming the cost of the object, the customer's materials are recognized as materials:

- provided for in the lists to the estimated norms for construction works at the site or in the statement of work volumes and resource consumption;

- purchased by the customer;

- transferred to the contractor to perform construction work on the site without transfer of ownership.

The customer's materials are accounted for by the contractor organization on off-balance sheet account 003 "Materials accepted for processing". The transfer of the customer's materials to the contracting organization for construction work at Profitagro LLC is formalized by a bill of lading TTN-1, or a bill of lading TN-2.

The following features shall be taken into account when executing these documents:

- in case of transfer of the Customer's materials for execution of works at the facility, the construction works of which are not subject to value added tax or are subject to value added tax partially, the name, quantity, price, cost of the material and the rate of value added tax at which the tax was paid by the Ordering Party when acquiring these materials shall be indicated;

- when transferring the customer's materials to perform work at the facility, the construction work of which is subject to value added tax, the name, quantity, price and cost of the material shall be indicated. The rate and amount of value added tax shall not be specified.

The value of the customer's materials to be transferred is determined at the value recorded in the customer's accounting records, taking into account the methods of valuation of materials on disposal.

For each transfer of customer materials (except for the transfer of materials from the customer to a general contractor), the organization must notify the receiving organization in writing of the basis and purpose of the transfer and confirm that the transferred materials belong to the customer's materials.

The cost of the customer's materials spent by the contracting organization in the performance of construction works is included by the customer in the cost of construction and installation works or works on installation of equipment in LLC Profitagro is reflected on debit of account 08 "Investments in long-term assets" and credit of account 07 "Equipment for installation and construction materials" (sub-account "Construction materials").

The article *"Materials"* in LLC "Profitagro" accounts for the cost of construction materials spent on the production of construction work according to the list provided by the estimated norms for construction, which is written off by accounting entry: on debit 08-1 "Acquisition of fixed assets. Formation of the main herd" and credit 07 "Equipment for installation and construction materials" - the cost of construction materials (cement) in the amount of RUR 98.77 was recognized.

Thus, synthetic accounting of investments in long-term assets in LLC Profitagro is kept in the General Ledger on account 08 "Investments in long-term assets". The register of analytical accounting is the Summary on account 08 "Investments in long-term assets". The register of statistical report is the annual report on commissioning of objects, fixed assets and use of investments in fixed assets. Entries in the report are made on the basis of primary documents (payment requests, invoices for the release of materials, cost allocation sheets).

2.3 Improvement of accounting for investments in non-current assets

In recent years, national accounting has been actively reformed and improved in order to bring it closer to International Financial Reporting Standards. The next step towards such convergence is the entry into force on January 1, 2013 of new instructions on accounting for long-term assets (fixed assets, intangible assets, investment real estate and long-term assets held for sale) [21].

The results of the conducted research allow us to make appropriate generalizations, conclusions and recommendations aimed at improving the accounting of investments in long-term assets in the researched LLC "Profitagro".

The logic of accounting records reflecting the process of depreciation accrual should be based on an assessment of the tendencies for an organization to receive income from the sale of products, the price of which includes depreciation charges.

LLC "Profitagro" uses a certain methodology in attributing depreciation charges:

attribution of depreciation charges to current expenses on ordinary activities of the organization. Application of such method of accounting of depreciation charges allows not only to reimburse the organization for the costs incurred for the acquisition (construction, manufacturing) of long-term tangible assets, but also to accumulate additional funds for the implementation of new capital investments. This method is very advantageous, because if during the period of depreciation the financial position of the organization is unstable, but there is a probability of its improvement in future periods, depreciation charges are recorded as deferred expenses.

The arrival of a period of stable income will allow to include deferred expenses in the expenses of the current period. In conditions of low demand for products, their competitiveness, in the absence of probability of receiving income from the sale of such products, it is advisable to include depreciation charges in the non-operating expenses of the organization.

This method of accounting records will allow to refuse from attributing depreciation charges to the sales price of products and form a more real financial result. However, in this case, depreciation charges will only represent a straight-line write-off of previously incurred costs associated with the acquisition of long-term tangible assets to the organization's losses.

For June 2017 in LLC "Profitagro" at the beginning of the month the depreciation of fixed assets was accrued for the total amount of 3,491,935.63 rubles, and at the end of the analyzed month - for 3,496,651, 40 rubles. According to the given data, it is possible to draw a conclusion that during the month the amount of depreciation was charged by 4 715, 77 rubles more than for the previous month. But the amount of written off depreciation of fixed assets for the analyzed period amounted to RUR 29,513.58. Only the car Lada-21214, Inv. No. 7/12 was written off in LLC "Profitagro" in June 2017.

Also, I would like to note that storing documents in the form of computer data on disk is certainly more expedient than storing them in the classical form, i.e. in the form of papers. It is much easier to find the necessary document, it is possible to store data for many years and not get confused in them, it is much easier to change any document, to draw up numerous references.

Profitagro LLC keeps accounting records partially according to the automated form of accounting with the use of 1C: Enterprise program complex. However, not all documents are kept in the automated form, which complicates their processing. In our opinion, we can conclude that it would be more appropriate to use an accounting automation system developed on the platform "1C", configuration "Chief Accountant" of the Belarusian firm "1C: Franchising LLC "Human Systems" in order to streamline reporting data on account 08 "Investment in Long-term Assets". This system is a universal system of automation of accounting and operational accounting of organizations of the Republic of Belarus, allows to carry out complex automation of practically all accounting areas, to perform the whole range of accounting tasks - from input of primary documents to reporting.

The system "1C: Enterprise" can be used to maintain any sections of accounting at enterprises of various types. The diverse and flexible capabilities of the system "1C: Enterprise" allow you to use it as a fairly simple and visual tool for accountants, and as a means of full automation of accounting from the input of primary documents to the formation of reports.

In our opinion, in order to improve the accounting of investments in long-term assets in LLC "Profitagro" it is necessary to form an Account Card. This document includes all accounting records with account 08 "Investments in long-term assets", and for each operation reflects the date of its occurrence, and the document on the basis of which the records were made. In addition, the account card shows the balances at the beginning and end of the period, the turnover for the period and the current balance after each transaction.

Since the account 08 "Investment in long-term assets" is analytically accounted for, it is possible to draw up a card reflecting accounting records only with specific objects of analytical accounting.

Thus, in LLC "Profitagro" automation of accounting of investments in long-term assets using the system "1C: Enterprise" will allow:

- reduce time and labor costs for document processing;

- to ensure the most complete and reliable accounting of investments in long-term assets for each object of expenditure, for the enterprise as a whole, both for a month and cumulatively from the beginning of the year;

- minimize the number of errors when transferring data from primary documents to synthetic and analytical accounting registers.

In the organization's practice, it is not uncommon to find transactions involving investments in non-current assets with long-term, multi-year installment payments. All the conditions for recognizing revenue from the sale of these assets are met. However, the assessment of receivables, the repayment of which is expected over a long period of time, at nominal value, does not reflect its real state and does not take into account all the ongoing inflationary processes. In these circumstances, it is necessary to take into account differences in the current and future value of cash flows and to include a time factor in the future value of receivables.

Information on long-term receivables, taking into account their discounted value, should be disclosed in the notes to the balance sheet and profit and loss statement. The use in analytical calculations of indicators of long-term receivables assessed at a discounted value will give a more complete and clear picture of the financial position of the organization, assess the liquidity of the organization's assets and its solvency.

When sales of tangible long-lived assets are made by installments over a long period of time, the problem arises as to the recognition of income and expenses in respect of the transaction. Since cash proceeds will be received over a long period of time and there is no definitive assurance that all cash will be received, recognition of income from the sale of such assets on an installment basis should be deferred. It is appropriate to recognize the gain on sale as deferred income (or deferred income). As cash payments for the sold asset are received, the deferred income will be recognized as operating income of the current period on a straight-line basis.

When long-term tangible assets are pledged as security for obligations under a loan or credit agreement, there is a high degree of credit and interest rate risk, and the resulting economic benefits to the entity in the form of cash inflows may be considered extraordinary.

The organization's obligations arising in connection with obtaining loans secured by real estate are obligations of a special kind, since they must be secured by the organization's real property. It is advisable to separate the obligations secured by mortgage from the total liabilities of the organization on separate sub-accounts of the first order "Mortgage Obligations" to the synthetic accounts of settlements on credits and loans, settlements with suppliers and contractors, settlements with various debtors and creditors. Analytical accounting should be kept by type of property pledged under the mortgage agreement. To account for the rights of the mortgagee arising upon receipt of real estate objects as a pledge, it is advisable to open a sub-account "Mortgage-backed loans" to the account "Financial Investments".

In our opinion, in LLC "Profitagro" it would be advisable to finalize the chart of accounts, open additional accounts and sub-accounts. For example, 08.2 - "Acquisition of land plots", since the organization does not have a separate sub-account. Also it would be necessary to allocate separately sub-account 08.3 - "Transfer of cattle from one herd to another" or 08.4 - "Acquisition of adult cattle", as the organization specializes in small-meat production. The major part is occupied by cattle breeding.

An important problem in accounting is the problem of "publicizing" the pledge transaction, warning creditors, future buyers and other persons about the right of the pledgee to the pledged property. In this connection the transferred objects of buyers and other persons about the right of the pledgee to the pledged property. In this connection, it is advisable to account for the pledged real estate objects on a separate sub-account "Fixed assets pledged" to the synthetic account "Fixed assets" on the basis of the value of the property recorded in the accounting of the pledging organization. The monetary value of pledged real estate may not coincide with the amount of the obligation secured by the mortgage. The value of the mortgaged property determined by agreement between the mortgagor and the mortgagee and corresponding to the mortgage agreement shall be recorded on the off-balance sheet account "Collateral for payments and obligations issued".

However, Profitagro LLC does not provide for such a sub-account, but we believe it would be appropriate to open one.

In determining the economic benefits of transferring real estate under a mortgage agreement, the mortgagor organization should compare the cash receipts and expenses associated with the mortgage. The amount and timing of mortgage interest expense can be anticipated more accurately than if the organization uses its own sources of financing to carry out its activities. The type of mortgage loan that provides for equal payments or variable payments allows for the determination of a fixed amount of interest on loans, which varies by type of mortgage.

It is advisable to record the costs associated with the fulfillment of obligations to pay interest that will be fulfilled in subsequent reporting periods on a separate balance sheet account "Upcoming expenses" in correspondence with the accounts for settlements on short-term and long-term credits and loans.

In contrast to deferred expenses, upcoming interest expenses on loans and borrowings are anti-cypical (anticipatory) expenses not actually incurred but recognized in the reporting period, and they relate to future reporting periods.

One of the problems of accounting for investments in long-term assets is housing construction.

Alymov Y., Levenkov N., Moiseychik G. argue that in order to solve the problem of involvement of citizens' monetary funds in housing construction and to create attractive conditions for investing citizens' own monetary funds in housing construction in the Republic of Belarus, the system of construction savings can be used [1].

In order for the system of housing savings to take root and work in Belarus, normal conditions for accumulation of investment resources should be created, first of all, inflation and, consequently, inflationary depreciation of savings should be suppressed, and incentives for investment use of profits and depreciation should be provided in the form of tax exemption of profits used for investment purposes.

Thus, the implementation of the proposed approaches to financing of the housing and construction complex will require the implementation of additional measures aimed at improving and developing mechanisms of crediting housing construction, creating institutions that allow for a wider use of alternative, off-budget sources, which, along with measures to reduce costs in construction, will make it possible to solve one of the most acute social problems - providing citizens of Belarus with comfortable housing in a shorter period of time.

In the course of systematic reforming of the accounting system of the Republic of Belarus in accordance with the International Financial Reporting Standards since January 1, 2013 a new accounting object - investment real estate - appeared in the domestic accounting [9].

Investment property is initially recognized at cost, including acquisition costs. Subsequently, investment property is stated at cost less accumulated depreciation and impairment losses. The cost of investment property acquired before January 1, 2015 is adjusted for inflation. Depreciation is charged on a straight-line basis over the estimated useful lives of 100 years.

The following factors must be met in order for real estate to be included in investment property:

- it must be rented out;

- the entity expects to obtain economic benefits associated with the immovable property;

- the value of the real property can be reliably determined.

The requirements to the content of information on investment real estate to be disclosed in the financial statements are defined in the Instruction on the procedure for preparation of financial statements approved by Resolution of the Ministry of Finance of the Republic of Belarus No. 111 dated 31.10.2011.

The value in use of investment property is the present (discounted) value of future cash flows from leasing out investment property and its disposal at the end of its useful life.

Thus, I would like to answer in general that in LLC "Profitagro" accounting of investments in long-term assets is conducted without significant problems and errors. It is improved by new developments, the organization strives for leading positions, for better accounting not only in the field of investments in long-term assets, but in general. They take into account all errors and nuances in documentation, strive to keep up with the leading organizations.

CHAPTER 3

ORGANIZATION OF CONTROL OVER INVESTMENTS IN LONG-LIVED ASSETS AND ITS IMPROVEMENT

3.1 Organization of internal control over investments in long-term assets

The successful operation of an organization requires a well-functioning management mechanism, the most important element of which is day-to-day internal control. Internal control is one of the main functions of management and is a system of constant monitoring and verification of the organization's work in order to ensure the validity and effectiveness of management decisions, to identify deviations and adverse situations, to inform the management in a timely manner to make decisions on the elimination, reduction and management of risks of its activities [2, p. 18-21].

Internal control is one of the functions of the management system, and therefore, the internal control system cannot be separated from the enterprise management system and its structure. An effective internal control system allows the management to be sure that the activities of the enterprise (organization) are conducted in accordance with the requirements of current legislation, approved policies and other directive and regulatory documents of the enterprise.

A significant contribution to the study of the problem of internal economic control made such domestic scientists as M. Belukha, F.F. Efimova, N. Vygovska, S.F. Golov, L.V. Dikan, E.V. Kalyuga, M.M. Kotsupatryi, L.V. Napadovs'ka, V.S. Rudnitsky, V.A. Shevchuk and other scientists.

The internal control of an agricultural enterprise can be characterized as a system functioning within the enterprise and as a management function, which is performed by the relevant departments, services or individuals in accordance with the duties assigned to them: agronomic, zooveterinary, engineering services, economic department and economist, chief accountant and accounting staff, materially responsible persons, management staff.

The leading place in the internal control of investments in long-term assets belongs to the employees of accounting services headed by the chief accountant of the enterprise [24].

The responsibilities of the chief accountant of Profitagro LLC in terms of internal control over investments in long-term assets include the following:

- strict compliance with all regulatory documents on accounting and financial reporting, as well as compliance with the principles of accounting organization of operations with investments in long-term assets, which are defined in the order on accounting policy of the enterprise;

- control over the timely and reliable recording of operations on the movement of investments in non-current assets, preparation of accounting registers and reflection of information on investments in non-current assets in financial statements;

- timely elimination of identified irregularities and deficiencies in accounting and reporting revealed by external and internal control;

- timely and reliable inventory of investments in non-current assets and recording of their results;

- providing methodological assistance to employees of the company's subdivisions on accounting, control and reporting of material resources.

The purpose of internal control of investments in long-term assets of LLC "Profitagro" is to ensure the safety of investments in long-term assets and their effective use, since investments in long-term assets are used in the main activities of the enterprise.

The main tasks of internal control of investments in long-term assets of LLC Profitagro are:

- control over the provision of design and estimate documentation for investments;

- control over the correctness and accuracy of record keeping;

- control over the correctness of determining the inventory value of construction objects put into operation and their entry into the fixed assets of the organization;

- control over timely, complete and accurate recognition of costs by type and object of investment in non-current assets;

- control over fulfillment of the plan of investments in long-term assets;

- control over correct organization of accounting and reporting on investment activities, etc.

The organization of internal control at LLC "Profitagro" is entrusted to the head of the enterprise, who through the available departments and individual employees controls the implementation of production plans and tasks, regulations, laws, instructions and his own orders. Therefore, for this purpose, enterprises usually issue an order "On the organization of accounting and control".

In the organization, control over the use of investments in long-term assets is carried out by conducting inventories of stocks, fixed assets and other property. Inventory of long-term assets is carried out at certain times by a special commission. The composition of the commission and the timing of the inventory are reflected in the inventory schedule, which is developed by the chief accountant and after review is approved by the head of the organization.

The present state of internal control of investments in long-term assets in LLC "Profitagro" allows us to conclude that it is necessary to develop and implement the provision and program of internal control.

The main load on implementation of internal control of investments in long-term assets in LLC "Profitagro" lies on the chief accountant, who ensure the organization of maintenance and verification of investments in long-term assets.

In general, it can be noted that the control system is effective, which is evident from a study of the inventory records of recent years and audit reports, in which no shortages or accounting errors were noted.

It is necessary that the control of the production process is carried out systematically in the interests of the enterprise, has a preventive and preventive orientation, i.e. it should identify deficiencies and weaknesses, the elimination of which improves the results compared to those achieved in its absence.

In our opinion, the system of internal economic control should be aimed at creating a system of compliance with the legislation of the Republic of Belarus in the sphere of financial activities, budget execution and internal procedures for compiling, reliability and improving the quality of financial statements and accounting, as well as improving the efficiency of the use of budget funds.

Thus, the control of investments in long-term assets plays a leading role in the organization. In order to increase the role of accounting and control in this case, it is necessary at the enterprise to observe the established document flow, to conduct timely control checks and inventories of long-term assets, to prevent significant deviations.

3.2 Procedure for auditing investments in non-current assets

Investments in long-term assets are the organization's expenses for the acquisition and creation of fixed assets, income investments in property and intangible assets, for the acquisition of property rights to land plots and natural resources, as well as expenses for research, development and technological work to create long-term assets.

The correctness of accounting and control of investments in long-term assets is of great importance and significantly affects the reliability of financial statements not only in the studied organization LLC "Profitagro", but also in all organizations as a whole, since currently there is a convergence of national accounting standards of long-term assets with the requirements of IFRS.

The sources of information for checking investments in long-term assets are: contracts for contracting and equipment supply; title lists of construction sites; logbook of completed construction and installation works (Form No. C-6); acceptance certificates of completed construction and installation works (Form No. C-2); certificates of cost of completed works and costs (Form No. C-3); primary documents on accounting of labor and its payment, consumption of materials; accounting registers - journal-orders No. 10-C, 11-C, statements No. 5-C "Settlements with customers (general contractors) and contractors (subcontractors) for work performed or relevant machine programs; statistical reporting "Report on the commissioning of facilities and the performance of contract work (form No. 1-KS (urgent)), etc.". [26, c. 169].

The proportionality of the sources of financing of investments in long-term assets and the volume of construction and installation works performed, costs for the acquisition of intangible assets and fixed assets ensures the preservation of own funds in circulation and financial stability of the organization.

Considering the control of investments in long-term assets in LLC "Profi-tagro", it should be noted that the audit is conducted general ledger, audit of accounting of income investments in tangible assets, disposal of fixed assets, verification of the correctness of depreciation reflection on fixed assets, verification of the order of annual inventory of fixed assets, verification of investments in long-term assets. In each item after the audit, violations are indicated, as well as recommendations for their correction. All of the above in the organization is reflected in the Report on the results of the audit.

Investments in long-term assets are checked in two directions [5, p. 83]:

- verification of investments in long-term assets related to new construction, reconstruction, expansion, technical re-equipment of existing fixed assets;

— verification of operations on acquisition (purchase) of fixed assets.

The audit of investments in non-current assets should begin with the study of contracts, agreements-contracts, commissioning act. Attention should be paid to the date of commissioning, signatures, useful life, correctness of accounting, correctness of depreciation and the order of its reflection in the accounting policy [34].

An audit of intangible assets should begin with an inventory of intangible asset documentation, i.e., verifying the existence of documents where each item is depicted or otherwise recorded.

The audit of fixed assets begins with the verification of contracts concluded with materially responsible persons. The auditor establishes the list of materially responsible persons at the enterprise for each object of fixed assets separately. The audit of fixed assets receipt begins with the study of documentation on the received fixed assets. The auditor pays attention to: date and correctness of depreciation accrual.

Particular attention in auditing investments in long-term assets should be paid to verifying the correctness of cost accounting, including capital investments in leased fixed assets provided for in the lease agreement.

Investments in long-term assets may be made at the expense of the lessor or at the expense of the lessee, as a reduction of rent. If the lease agreement provides for investments in non-current assets in leased fixed assets at the expense of the lessee, then at the end of the lease term they are transferred to the lessor free of charge, and entries are made in the accounting records on the free of charge transfer of fixed assets.

When checking the correctness of cost accounting for investments in long-term assets, it is necessary to establish [5,p. 116-117]:

— the way in which investments are utilized;

— correctness of documentation of the volumes of performed construction and installation works and their reflection in accounting in case of contractual method of work;

— the correctness of recognizing expenses on other capital works and costs;

— correctness of cost recognition in the accounting of costs under the economic method of work;

— correctness of allocation of costs to the costing items forming the actual cost of construction and installation works and finished construction products.

When starting to examine investments in long-term assets, it is necessary to establish the method by which the investments are developed. When investments are developed by the contracting method, it is necessary to verify the correctness of recording costs according to the data of primary documents. For this purpose it is necessary to keep in mind that the developer (investor), performing works by the contracting method, accounts for the costs at the estimated (contractual) cost of work performed. For accounting of investments in long-term assets in LLC Profitagro, as noted earlier, account 08 "Investments in long-term assets" is used.

The investor records costs on this account on the basis of payment instructions submitted for payment by design and contractor construction organizations. Contractor construction organizations should attach certificates (Form No. 3) on the cost of completed works and expenses to the invoices.

Next, it is necessary to determine the correctness of recognizing expenditures for other capital works and costs. These include[13, pp. 401-402]:

— design and survey works, as well as author's supervision of design organizations;

— costs of land acquisition and resettlement in connection with construction;

– costs of maintenance of the Directorates of enterprises under construction and technical supervision;

– expenses related to the application of additional payments, benefits and advantages established by the government, which are not included in the unit rates for construction work and in price lists for installation work, paid under separate invoices (allowances for mobile and traveling nature of work; allowances for length of service, etc.), and other work and expenses.

When works are carried out by the economic method, developers (customers) also record the costs incurred on account 08 "Investments in long-term assets" not at the estimated cost, but at actual cost. Account 08 "Investments in Long-Term Assets" in this case has a costing nature. In accounting, the same primary documents and accounting registers are used to record business operations as in the accounting of contracting organizations.

The level of costs of construction and installation works is directly related to the volume of work performed. Therefore, as a rule, in the course of the audit, control measurements of construction and assembly works performed at construction-in-progress facilities are carried out, with the help of which additions to the volumes of construction and assembly works performed, and, accordingly, illegal writing-off of construction materials and structures, and overpayment of wages are established.

Construction and installation organizations investing in long-term assets under contractual agreements, the costs of construction and installation works are accounted for in advance on account 20 "Main production" and as they are delivered to the customer are written off to account 90 "Income and expenses on current activities". In this case, it is necessary to establish the correctness of assignment of costs to costing items (materials; basic wages of workers; costs of operation of construction machinery and mechanisms; overheads), forming the actual cost of construction and installation works and finished construction products.

Profitagro LLC was audited in 2016. No violations were identified during the audit.

Thus, during the audit of investments in long-term assets, it is necessary to establish the efficiency of the use of funds allocated for capital investments; timeliness, completeness and reliability of accounting for capital investment costs.

3.3 Improvement of control over investments in non-current assets

Special attention should be paid to the company's accounting reports, improvement and development of investments in long-term assets, as well as their control.

In our opinion, the persons responsible for conducting an audit should analyze the identified violations, determine their causes and develop proposals for taking measures to eliminate and prevent them in the future.

Employees of the organization who have committed deficiencies, misrepresentations and violations must provide the Director with written explanations on issues related to the results of the control. Based on the results of the audit of investments in non-current assets, the Director, together with chief specialists, should develop an action plan to eliminate the identified deficiencies and violations, specifying deadlines and responsible persons.

The correctness of determining the planned cost of construction, acquisition of facilities and other investments in long-term assets should be checked separately. For this purpose, it is necessary to establish the reasonableness of the application of estimated rates, contract prices, planned cost of works performed by economic method, breeding of repair stock, etc.

When checking the feasibility of investments for the purchase of machinery and equipment, it is necessary to establish the actual availability of appropriate equipment in the farm, planned and actual work volumes, the average output of certain types of machinery and equipment, the real need and funding [32].

It is also necessary to check separately the correctness of determining the planned cost of construction, acquisition of objects and other investments in long-term assets. For this purpose it is necessary to establish the validity of application of estimated rates, contract prices, growing of repair youngsters, planned cost of works performed by economic method, etc.

Separately, it is necessary to check compliance with the established procedure for acceptance into operation of acquired and completed construction of fixed assets, the correctness of determining the inventory value of objects, the timeliness of their receipt on the balance sheet of the farm.

According to the results of the audit conducted at Profitagro LLC, we can note that the problem of accounting for investments in long-term assets is the inattention with which managers treat accounting.

It is necessary to introduce additional control over accounting for investments in long-term assets on the part of the company's management. This means familiarization of the manager with accounting documents, his study of the regulations in force in this area. In our opinion, such an approach will make it possible to spend funds for the acquisition of long-term assets more rationally and increase the discipline of their use by the employees of the enterprise.

In addition, in our opinion, it is necessary to introduce an analysis of the efficiency of the use of investments in long-term assets based on accounting data under the direct control of the head of the enterprise. In this case, the manager will receive a more complete picture of the state of affairs at the enterprise.

It is also necessary to develop a program of internal control in LLC "Profitagro". It should be a functional-organizational aggregate of control environment, including objects, subjects of control, information support system, represented by accounting and internal reporting and its method, combining the appropriate ways and techniques of studying the objects of control using a significant nomenclature of accounting and control procedures.

Each structural element of the system of internal control should be considered both separately and in the aggregate. At the same time, the initial premise is an indisputable statement that internal control is available in any economic entity where economic activity is carried out and resources (labor, material, financial) are used. But the level of its organization will be different, and this will depend primarily on the formed control environment (basic conditions). The main conditions are currently recognized as: style and basic principles of management of the organization, distribution of responsibility and authority, personnel policy, organizational structure.

We believe that this list of facts should also be supplemented with such facts as technological features of the business entity and the degree of participation of the owner in the management and leadership of the organization, economic stability in the field of activity (brand awareness of the enterprise, image), changes in tax policy, development of legislative and regulatory framework.

The degree of owners' participation in the management of the organization's activities is one of the most important conditions for the formation of the system of internal economic control. Owners (or their representatives) are interested in a high level of functioning of this system. In all other cases, its level will always be lower, so we can indicate a direct correlation between the level of the internal control system and the degree (representation) of participation of owners in the activities of the organization.

Thus, one of the constituent elements of the system of internal control should be the accounting system, which forms the information necessary for control. Therefore, without the organized functioning of the accounting system it is impossible to form a system of internal control.

So, in order to streamline specific techniques and procedures in the system of internal control on account 08 "Investments in long-term assets" we propose in LLC "Profitagro" to use the program of internal control (Annex 1).

Regulations on internal control allows to streamline and more clearly delimit the work in the field of control between departments and services of the farm. Duplication and parallelism in the work of planning and economic, accounting services give rise to serious shortcomings in the organization of control. One of the reasons for the shortcomings in the organization and practice of control is that many important theoretical issues of this complex management function have not yet been thoroughly investigated.

To improve internal control of investments in long-term assets, the chief accountant is recommended to conduct an annual analysis of the efficiency of their use, which will help to identify active and inactive facilities, the efficiency of their use in the production process, their provision of the farm. For the identified inactive facilities, the possibilities of bringing them into operation and measures to be taken by the farm for this purpose are studied.

The main methods of control over the use of long-term assets are the methods of economic analysis, with the help of which private indicators of the use of individual types of assets (buildings, structures, trucks, machinery and tractor fleet, etc.) are determined, as well as general indicators characterizing the efficiency of the use of all fixed assets (stock return on the value of gross output and profit per unit of assets, coefficients of their disposal and renewal, the degree of wear and tear).

The use of the proposed ways of improvement will significantly improve the control of investments in long-term assets not only in the organization under study LLC "Profitagro", but also in agricultural organizations of the Republic of Belarus as a whole.

CONCLUSION

Summarizing the work, the following conclusions can be drawn. The purpose of this work has been achieved and the tasks have been solved. The most important issues of this topic have been disclosed.

In the theoretical part of the study, the concept and role of investment in long term assets were defined.

All assets of Profitagro LLC are either classified as long-term investments (investments) or are included in inventories. In the world practice it is considered that long-term assets are long-term deferred expenses. If they pay for themselves quickly in economic activity, it is more profitable to write them off within a short period of operation and purchase new objects.

Fixed and intangible assets need periodic modernization and replacement. Production of new products, development of new markets, expansion of the enterprise's activities require investment in long-term assets. Of course, if a completely new line of activity is created or even a new line of activity is separated into a newly created subsidiary organization, investments should be made not only in long-term assets, but also in current assets of the new enterprise. Nevertheless, for an enterprise making investments in the authorized capital of a subsidiary organization, these investments are long-term financial investments, i.e. long-term assets.

As a rule, in the majority of production enterprises, as well as in the studied LLC Profitagro, a significant part of property belongs to long-term assets, and the overwhelming part of investments in long-term assets is fixed assets. Fixed assets are one of the most important factors of any production. Their condition and effective utilization directly affects the final results of economic activity of enterprises.

In the second chapter of the research work was carried out accounting of investments in long-term assets of LLC "Profitagro".

In the course of accounting of investments in long-term assets it was found out that LLC "Profitagro" maintains various primary documents on receipt, movement and disposal of investments in long-term assets.

Analytical accounting on sub-accounts is carried out by costs associated with the formation of the main herd and types of animals (cattle (pigs, horses, etc.).

The peculiarity of accounting for perennial plantings is that on the analytical accounts opened before the fruiting period the costs are accounted for within a calendar year, so annually at the end of the reporting period they are written off by accumulating total to debit account 01 "Fixed assets", analytical account "Young plantings", credit sub-account 08-5 "Acquisition and creation of other long-term assets".

Thus, the correspondence of account 08 "Investments in Long-Term Assets" with other accounts is established in accordance with Annex 8 to this Instruction.

The results of the conducted research allow us to make appropriate generalizations, conclusions and recommendations aimed at improving the accounting of investments in long-term assets in the research enterprise LLC "Profitagro".

In case of stable dynamics of income from sales, it is advisable to include depreciation charges in the current expenses on ordinary activities of the organization. Application of such methodology of accounting of depreciation charges will allow not only to reimburse organizations for the costs incurred for the acquisition (construction, manufacturing) of long-term tangible assets, but also to accumulate additional funds for new capital investments. If the financial position of an organization is unstable during the period of depreciation accrual, but there is a probability of its improvement in future periods, depreciation charges should be recorded as deferred expenses.

In the course of systematic reforming of the accounting system of the Republic of Belarus in accordance with the International Financial Reporting Standards, a new object of accounting - investment real estate - appeared in domestic accounting since January 1, 2013.

Investment property is initially recognized at cost, including acquisition costs. Subsequently, investment property is stated at cost less accumulated depreciation and impairment losses. The cost of investment property acquired before January 1, 2015 is adjusted for inflation. Depreciation is charged on a straight-line basis over the estimated useful lives of 100 years.

In the third chapter of the work the organization of control of investments in long-term assets is considered and recommendations for its improvement in LLC "Profitagro" are offered.

In the organization, control over the use of investments in non-current assets is carried out by conducting inventories of fixed assets, inventories and other property. Inventory of non-current assets is carried out by a special commission at certain dates. The timing of the inventory and the composition of the commission are reflected in the inventory schedule. This schedule is developed by the chief accountant and after review is approved by the head of the organization.

The present state of internal control of investments in long-term assets in LLC "Profitagro" allows us to conclude that it is necessary to develop and implement the provision and program of internal control.

The main load on implementation of internal control of investments in long-term assets in LLC "Profitagro" lies on the chief accountant, who ensure the organization of maintenance and verification of investments in long-term assets.

In general, it can be noted that the control system is effective, which is evident from a study of the inventory records of recent years and audit reports, in which no shortages or accounting errors were noted.

It is necessary to introduce additional control over accounting for investments in long-term assets on the part of the company's management. This means familiarization of the manager with accounting documents, his study of the regulations in force in this area. Such an approach will make it possible to spend funds more rationally on the acquisition of long-term assets and increase the discipline of their use by the enterprise's employees.

Also, in order to streamline specific techniques and procedures in the system of internal control on account 08 "Investment in long-term assets" in LLC "Profitagro" we propose to use the program of internal control.

Thus, using these recommendations in practice, the management and accounting service of LLC "Profitagro" could always have a real idea of the effectiveness of investments in long-term assets of the enterprise, ahead of the consequences of their unprofitability, not waiting until the manufactured products fill the warehouses of the enterprise.

LIST OF REFERENCES

1. Alymov, Y., Levenkov, N., Moiseychik, G. Housing construction: new approaches / Y. Alymov, N. Levenkov, G. Moiseychik // Bank Bulletin - 2013. - № 25. - C. 4-13.

2. Belyaev, I. I. I., Korobova N. M. / Improving the system of internal economic control in JSC "Goretskoe" Goretsky district of Mogilev region // Scientific search of the youth of the XXI century Collection of scientific articles on the materials of the XVI International Scientific Conference of students and graduate students // EE "Belarusian State Agricultural Academy". - Gorki, 2016. - 186 c.

3. Bepersch, T.I. Classification of long-term assets [Electronic resource] / T.I. Bepersch // BNTU.by. - Mode of access: http://www.bntu.by/news/67- conference-mido/3266-2015-11-30-16-14-48.html. - Date of access: 20.07.2017.

4. Accounting accounting of investments in long-term assets [Electronic resource] / Studfiles.net. - Access mode: https://studfiles.net/preview/56307- 78/page:4/. - Date of access: 01.08.2017.

5. Verenich, G. D. Revision and audit : textbook / G. D. Verenich [et al]; ed. by G. D. Verenich, E. N. Verbitskaya, I. V. Shcherbakova. - Minsk: BNTU, 2013. - 162 c.

6. Gridyushko, E. N., Ermolitskaya, O. V. / Accounting of investment real estate in accordance with IFRS // International Scientific and Practical Conference "Management of socio-economic systems and legal research: theory, methodology and practice" // Bryansk State University named after Academician I. G. Petrovsky Institute of Economics and Law. - Bryansk, 2017.

7. Documenting and accounting of long-term assets [Electronic resource] / Student Library Online. - Mode of access:yr:/Sh^bio- oks .net/1374653/buhgalte-rskiy_uchet_i_audit/dokumentalnoe_oformlenie_uchet_- dolgosrochnyh_aktivov. - Date of access: 01.08.2017.

8. Long-term assets [Electronic resource] / Allbest.ru. - Access mode: http://revolution.allbest.ru/audit/00284473_0.html. - Date of access: 28.07.2017.

9. Ermolitskaya, O. V. / Practice of application of assessment and accounting of investment real estate in the Republic of Belarus // Finance: theoretical aspects, problems and prospects of development Collection of scientific articles on the materials of the V-th scientific-practical conference // EE "Belarusian State Agricultural Academy". - Gorki, 2017. - C.

10. Foreign investments in January-June 2017 [Electronic resource] / National Statistical Committee of the Republic of Belarus. - Access mode: http://www.belstat.-gov.by/ofitsialnayastatistika/makroekonomika-i-okru-zhayushchaya-

sreda/finansy/operativnaya-informatsiya_14/ob-inostrannyh-inves- titsiyah2/. - Date of access: 20.07.2017.

11. Klippert, E.N. Accounting : textbook / E.N. Klippert, A.S. Chechetkin. Klippert, A.S. Chechetkin. - Minsk : Register, 2014. - 448 c.

12. Kutselai, E.V. Accounting and control of investments in long-term assets / E.V. Kutselai, T.E. Ruban // Accounting and analysis of economic activity in the agricultural sector and its financial support Collection of scientific articles on the materials of the XVI International Scientific Conference of students and graduate students // EE "Belarusian State Agricultural Academy". - Gorki, 2015. - 186 C.

13. Makeenko, G. I. Methods of research of economic operations in construction by an expert-accountant [Electronic resource]. - Mode of access: http://www.bseu.by:8080/bit-stream/edoc/58968/1/Makeenko_G._I..pdf. - Date of access: 07.08.2017.

14. International Financial Reporting Standards // Analytical legal system "Business-info" [Electronic resource]. - 2017. - Access mode: www.bisiness-info.by. - Date of access: 18.08.2017.

15. International Accounting Standard (IAS) 16 "Property, Plant and Equipment" [Electronic resource] / minfin.ru. - Access mode: https://www.min- fin.ru/common-/upload/library/2015/01/main/IAS16.pdf. -Date of access: 22.07.2017.

16. International Accounting Standard (IAS) 17 "Leases" [Electronic resource] / minfin.ru. - Access mode: https://www.minfin.ru/- common/upload/library-/no_date/2012/ias_17.pdf. - Date of access: 23.07.2017.

17. International Accounting Standard (IAS) 20 "Accounting for Government Grants and Disclosure of Government Assistance" [Electronic resource] / minfin.ru. - Access mode: https://www.minfin.ru/com- mon/upload/library/no_date/2013/ias-_20.pdf. - Date of access: 23.07.2017.

18. International Accounting Standard (IAS) 23 "Borrowing Costs" [Electronic resource] / minfin.ru. - Access mode: https : //www. minfin.ru/common-/upload/library/no_date/2013/IAS_23 .pdf. - Date of access: 23.07.2017.

19. International Financial Reporting Standard (IFRS) 5 "Non-current Assets Held for Sale and Discontinued Operations". [Electronic resource] / minfin.ru. - Access mode: https://www.min- fin.ru/common/upload/library/2014/02/main/-IFRS_05_-36n.pdf. -Date of access: 22.07.2017.

20. IAS 40 "Investment Property". [Electronic resource] / Studfiles.net. - Access mode: https://studfiles.net/preview/3178691/page:30/. - Date of access: 29.07.2017.

21. New in accounting of long-term assets [Electronic resource] / BelTA. News of Belarus. - Access mode: http://m/belta.by/ onlinecon- ference/view/novoe-v-buhgalterskom-uchete-dolgosrochnyh-aktivov-588. - Date of access: 12.08.2017.

22. On issues of accrual of depreciation of fixed assets and intangible assets in 2017 [Electronic resource]: Resolution of the Council of Ministers of the Republic of Belarus, January 30, 2017, No. 84 // Kodeksy-by.com. 2017, № 84 // Kodeksy-by.com. - Mode of access: http://kodeksyby.com/norm -_akt/source-CM%20RB/type - Resolution/84-30.01.2017.yt. - Date of access: 22.07.2017.

23. About establishing the forms of primary documents in construction [Electronic resource]: Resolution of the Ministry of Architecture and Construction of the Republic of Belarus, April 29, 2011, № 13 // Law Legislation of the Republic of Belarus. 2011, № 13 // Law Legislation of the Republic of Belarus. - Access mode: http://www.levonevski.net/pravo/norm2013/num- 09/d09785.html. - Date of access: 02.08.2017.

24. Organization and state of intrafarm control of long-term biological assets [Electronic resource] / Student library online. - Mode of access: http://studbooks.net/1389449/buhgalterskiy_uchet_i_- audit/organizatsiya_sostoyanie_vnutrihozyaystvennogo_kontrolya_dolgosrochnyh_bi ologicheskih_aktivov. - Date of access: 13.08.2017.

25. Fixed assets of the Republic of Belarus [Electronic resource] / National Statistical Committee of the Republic of Belarus. - Access mode: http://www.belstat.gov.by/- ofitsialnaya-statistika/makroekonomika-i-okruzhayush-   chaya-sreda/finansy/godovyedannye-_14/osnovnye-sredstva-respubliki-belarus_/. - Date of access: 24.07.2017.

26. Pavlovich, T. P. Revision and audit : answers to exam questions / T. P. Pavlovich, E. G. Pavlovich. - Minsk :TetraSystems, 2009. - 240 c.

27. Ponomarenko, P. G. Accounting: textbook for universities / P. G. Ponomarenko. - Minsk: Vysheyshaya Shkola, 2013.

28. The concept of investments in long-term assets, their classification, accounting tasks [Electronic resource] / Lectures. Com. - Mode of access: http://lek- tsii.com/2-5374.html. - Date of access: 25.07.2017.

29. The concept and types of investments in long-term assets and the tasks of their accounting [Electronic resource] / My Library. - Access mode: http://mybiblioteka. su/1-67343.html. - Date of access: 15.07.2017.

30. The concept, essence, classification of long-term assets and tasks of their accounting [Electronic resource] /Studopedia.ru. - Mode of access: yyr:///z1:iyo-

pedia.ru/13_157485-_razdel-.html. - Date of access: 28.07.2017.

31. Rybak, T., Naumchik, O. Mandatory audit: what will be checked? // Chief Accountant. - 2013. - № 24. - C. 112.

32. Topic 1 Theoretical foundations of economic control [Electronic resource] / Studmed.ru. - Access mode: http://www.studmed.ru/view/lekcii-po- discipline-kontrol-i-reviziya-2011-god_7f499d8.html. - Date of access: 09.08.2017.

33. Topic 14. Investments and increasing their efficiency [Electronic resource]: a course of lectures / Studfiles.net. - Access mode: https://studfiles.net-/preview/3104529/. - Date of access: 28.07.2017.

34. Topic 6: Audit of long-term assets [Electronic resource] / Studo-pediYa. - Mode of access: http://studopedia.su/4_2381_tema--audit-dolgosrochnih- aktivov.html. - Date of access: 09.08.2017.

35. Chechetkin, A. S. Accounting and audit: textbook / A. S. Chechetkin, S. A. Chechetkin. - Minsk : data-processing center of the Ministry of Finance, 2017. - 552 c.

36. Shcherbatyuk, S.Y. International standards of accounting, financial reporting and audit: a lecture note for specialties. 1-25 01 08 Accounting, analysis and audit / S.Y. Scherbatyuk; Grodno State Agrarian University. - Grodno. - 2010. - 156 c.

APPENDIX

Program of internal control on account 08 "Investments in long-term assets"

Name of procedure	Section of the internal control system	Inspection deadlines	Performers
Examination of the procedure for utilization of fixed assets transferred from the structure of income investments	Verification of property, plant and equipment	once a year	Manager, Chief Accountant
Procedure for forming the cost of the leased item	Verification of property, plant and equipment	Upon receipt of leasing objects	Chief Accountant
Compliance of the terms of putting the leased property on the balance sheet with the terms of the lease agreement	Verification of property, plant and equipment	Upon receipt of leasing objects	Chief Accountant
Evaluation of information on availability of inseparable improvements of leased (leased) property	Verification of property, plant and equipment	once a year	Chief Accountant
Review of operations for timeliness and reasonableness of write-off of fixed assets at the end of the lease agreement	Verification of property, plant and equipment	Upon write-off of fixed assets	Chief Accountant
Verification of the correctness of the inclusion of assets in the equipment to be installed	Verification of investments in non-current assets	once a year	Fixed Assets Accountant
Verification of documentary evidence of transfer of property for installation	Verification of investments in non-current assets	once a year	Fixed Assets Accountant
Verification of accounting of expenses related to acquisition of fixed assets	Verification of investments in non-current assets	Upon acquisition of fixed assets	Chief Accountant
Verification of classification of expenses on restoration of fixed assets	Verification of investments in non-current assets	once a year	Fixed Assets Accountant
Request for provision of information on ongoing OS restorations	Verification of investments in non-current assets	Upon recovery of fixed assets	Chief Accountant
Availability of defect documentation for fixed assets transferred for restoration	Verification of investments in non-current assets	Upon recovery of fixed assets	Chief Accountant

Note: Proprietary development.

I want morebooks!

Buy your books fast and straightforward online - at one of world's fastest growing online book stores! Environmentally sound due to Print-on-Demand technologies.

Buy your books online at
www.morebooks.shop

Kaufen Sie Ihre Bücher schnell und unkompliziert online – auf einer der am schnellsten wachsenden Buchhandelsplattformen weltweit! Dank Print-On-Demand umwelt- und ressourcenschonend produziert.

Bücher schneller online kaufen
www.morebooks.shop

Printed by Books on Demand GmbH, Norderstedt / Germany